TWO PLAYS

James Purdy

New London Press / *Dallas, Texas*

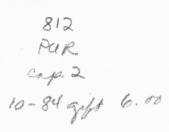

FIRST PRINTING

ISBN 0-89683-001-2
ISBN 0-89683-003-9 (limited edition)
Manufactured in the United States

A DAY AFTER THE FAIR

SCENE ONE

A dilapidated unfurnished room in a lonely city near which loom up enormous skyscrapers and bridges.
There are two straight-backed chairs facing the audience. In the rear, a small bed, with a stand on which rests a water-pitcher. Two Clowns live here, brothers.
NEIL, *the younger of the two brothers, is discovered playing with a pack of cards at a little tabouret which he has suddenly fished up and placed before the chair on which he is accustomed to sit.*

NEIL: *(Shakes his head)* I can't get the cards to say anything today. . .What's amiss? *(Puts down the pack, then begins to re-shuffle.)* If Arnold would only come back. . .It's not right he leaves me alone so many hours of the day. . .And I could just as well go out on the street with him and perform my part of the act too, like in old times. . .But wait. . .What are the cards trying to tell me now? *(He looks mesmerized at the cards lying spread out on the table.)* They are trying to warn me? Or are they saying *Ask no more, little Neil, ask no more. . .*No more, then! *(Throws the cards on the floor, and sobs.)* No, no, they can't mean what they said! *(Stares down at the cards.)* I could never harm any-body!. . .I'll tell you what. . .I'll put on my Clown's face too, though Arnold's forbidden it. . .And it will make me lose the blues. . .Why shouldn't I put on my Clown's face. I was a Clown just like him. *(Goes to the rear, and brings a box of makeup.)* I don't even need to look in a mirror to know how. . .Could do it in the dark! That was when we was both alive all right, like Arnold always says. . .*(He quickly makes his face up as a specter-clown.)*

(A loud arhythmic knock repeated three times is heard on the outside door.)

NEIL: *(Terrified)* Arnold warned me not to answer. . .Holy Jesus! *(Bows his head. . .The knock is repeated, louder.)* It can't be him. Can't be Oswin. . .Arnold's forbidden him ever to see me. . .

OSWIN: *(Calls from outside)* I know you're in there, Neil, and I know you're alone. So open up for me. . .

NEIL: You know what Arnold said he would do to you if you called here again, Oswin. . .So go away, please. . .You know too Arnold will beat me if he knows I have talked with you. . .So please go before he returns. . .I cannot bear the weight of his fists again! *(Cries.)* Go now while the coast's clear.

OSWIN: I will never go away until I have seen you, so open the door. . .I've something special to tell you. . .

NEIL: *(Rises slowly and stumbles, for the tears and the paint have obscured his vision. He goes toward the door.)* Come in then, if you have to, Oswin.

(OSWIN enters, embraces NEIL.)

OSWIN: He cannot keep you from me, Neil. . .Never, never. . .But oh, my God, why have you put on your clown paint again! Don't you remember, I told you I don't want you to be a clown again. . .Never!

NEIL: *(Plaintive)* But I miss it. . .I miss the circus. . .More than Arnold does. *(To himself)* I was more the real clown! *(To OSWIN)* Yes, I miss it more than Arnold does. . .After all he can go out on the streets and do his act and collect money. . .

OSWIN: As if Arnold needed money! I know he is rich. He is rotten with money. Yet see how he lives! See how he keeps you!. . .If you will run off with me, Neil, you can live like a young prince. . .I have told you that a thousand times to your deaf ears. . .Why do you cling to this Arnold! You will always live like a castoff while you do. Come with me, and you will be. . .

NEIL: I am a clown and the brother of a clown.

OSWIN: You told me once, and not too long ago, either, that you loved me.

NEIL: I do Oswin. . .I am sure I do.

OSWIN: Well, then, pack your things. You have so little, actually, and come along with me. . .We'll go far enough. . .I have money, Neil. . .Scads. . .

NEIL: I said I was a clown at heart, and I need to live with Arnold. . .We are the only clowns! My father was a clown, and his father. And before him my great grandfather was a juggler. We have always followed the circus.

OSWIN: But you don't now! The Clown Master fired the both of you! You lost your profession forever!

NEIL: Stop, stop! You must stop!

OSWIN: Tell you what, Neil. I am going to wash off your paint, and talk to you soft. . .Remember how you told me you liked my soft-talking.

NEIL: I do, I do. I love you Oswin. . .But if Arnold should come in! He would. . .

OSWIN: I am more of a man than ten Arnolds! Where is the warm water, and the yellow soap.

(OSWIN goes back to a small sink and prepares a basin of soapy water. He returns and begins washing NEIL. Finally he removes his shirt, but before he begins to bathe his chest, he kisses him like one famished, and then bathes him cautiously over his chest, and under his arms, stopping every now and then to embrace him.)

NEIL: Oh, Oswin, when you put your lips on my flesh I seem to turn to nothing! I feel like a cloud that is drifting away.

OSWIN: Now I have washed off your circus paint, walk out of here with me. Now! Now!

(ARNOLD has entered, unseen by the others, and is watching them with poorly controlled fury. ARNOLD is of massive build, in contrast to NEIL and OSWIN, who though strong men, are like midgets in comparison with him. ARNOLD is painted as a clown.)

ARNOLD: I turn my back for one moment, and see what comes in from the rat's nest.

OSWIN: This is none of your affair now, Arnold. Neil is coming with me. . .

ARNOLD: *(Maniacal)* Neil does nothing without he gets word from me. . .Set him straight, Neil.

NEIL: I don't know what to say, Arnold.

ARNOLD: *(Strikes NEIL, knocking him down.)* Talk like that again to me, and see what you get then.

(OSWIN strikes ARNOLD, a scuffle follows, and ARNOLD overpowers OSWIN, but only after considerable effort. . . NEIL is whimpering in a corner to which he has crawled, and wiping the blood from his face. . .ARNOLD approaches him, breathing hard.)

ARNOLD: Why do you bring out the worst in me? How can you even allow another person to say he is taking you away from me? Sometimes I think you do not realize that you are my brother and can never leave me, and that we are clowns. We are brothers, but above all we are clowns. . .

NEIL: *(Passionately)* Were, Arnold, were!

ARNOLD: *(Choking NEIL)* Don't you ever utter that statement again in my presence! Hear?

(At this moment he is aware OSWIN is approaching him with a knife drawn. ARNOLD seizes him perfunctorily, disarms him, and throws him to the floor.)

ARNOLD: *(To NEIL)* See what you'd be running off with? A

Two Plays

common cutthroat, but he can only kill behind your back. . .*(To
OSWIN)* If you ever come here again, it will be your last visit to
anybody on this earth. *(Kneeling over OSWIN's prostrate form,
and toying with the knife about his throat)* But wait a minute,
wait. . .You might be useful to us yet. . .Even you might be of
some real everyday use. . .Are you agreeable to a bargain, or
shall I finish you off?

OSWIN: Go on, why don't you kill me?

ARNOLD: Because I've thought of something better. . .Tell
me the truth. . .They say you've killed men before. . .

OSWIN: *(Contemptuous)* What of it?

ARNOLD: Aha. He admits it. . .Just like that. . .See who
you have been so close to, Neil. . .A confessed cutthroat as well
as a reputed one! All right. All right!

NEIL: Let him go, Arnold. You've punished him enough.

ARNOLD: Never. He will come in handy, he has come in
handy. . .Oswin, I need you for a job. You can do it. *(Threatens
him by touching the blade again to his throat.)*

OSWIN: *(Spits in ARNOLD's face.)* You has-been clown.
Kill me, why don't you. You don't have the balls.

ARNOLD: *(Releasing him)* Do you know why we have come
down in the world, Oswin? From being famous clowns, to this!
*(The knife is still in his hand, he waves his arm about the squalor
of the room.)* From known artists to street beggars! Who is the
author of our ruin?

OSWIN: *(Frightened by his rage.)* The Clown Master, I
suppose.

ARNOLD: You suppose, you cocksucker. You know. You
know it.

OSWIN: All right, all right, Arnold. The Clown Master ruined
you.

ARNOLD: Make it stronger. Whip me with the words.

OSWIN: He framed you. He sent you down the river.

ARNOLD: And why, Oswin, was he so lavish with ruin?

OSWIN: Because he loved your brother Neil and you
withheld that prize from him.

7

James Purdy

ARNOLD: *(Stung by the truth.)* Now that you've said it, shut up. . .*(Holds* OSWIN's *mouth shut with his hand.)* Never say it again.

OSWIN: *(Struggling free)* You bawled for the truth, you crumb, and now I'm to be beaten again for giving it to you.

ARNOLD: Very well, then. Repeat and tell again all you know. Spare me no torture.

OSWIN: *(Rising and staring at* ARNOLD *balefully)* The Clown Master envied you, then. He loved both of you actually. He loved your souls as much or more than your bodies, but you were both marble. You both indeed lived—in another world to which no other human being can gain admission. Talk of forbidden sins and crimes without a name! Were there ever such sinners as you two!

ARNOLD: *(Drops the knife.)* Go on. Tear my heart out. . .

OSWIN: *(Picks up the knife and puts it away in his breast pocket.)* The Clown Master ruining you was the only way he could approach you.

ARNOLD: Go on.

OSWIN: And so after you had closed the last of all the doors on him, you found yourselves street beggars. Street beggars in paint!

ARNOLD: *(Pointing to his heart)* Cut it out and throw it to the dogs, you pool of poisoned puke! *(Weeps deliriously. . .then comes to himself.)* Listen, Oswin. *(Begins almost to caress him.)* I take back all I have said against you.

OSWIN: Get your crazy hands off me! If you touch me again, I'll mangle you.

ARNOLD: As if I cared about that. . .No, no, I take back all the bad things I said against you, Oswin my friend. . .let me instead praise you. . .How do you want me to praise you?

OSWIN: *(Disgusted, fearful)* You are insane. In-sane! Let me get out of here. . .And keep him. *(Staring at* NEIL*)* Keep him!

ARNOLD: *(Detaining* OSWIN*)* Listen first, Oswin. . .Listen carefully and good. . .

OSWIN: I want out of here. Away from a diseased hyena like you.

8

ARNOLD: Look, call me anything you like. See?. . .Beat me, if you like. . .I can take it. Strike me, Oswin, go on, I promise not to strike back. . .Go on, hit me.
OSWIN: *(Suspicious)* No.
ARNOLD: Go on. Use your fists. Sock me
OSWIN: *(As if hypnotized)* Yeah?
ARNOLD: Strike me. Hard. *(Takes off his shirt.)* Go on, beat me all you wish, for I've a favor to ask of you.

(OSWIN, fascinated, languidly hits ARNOLD once.)

ARNOLD: Hit me harder. See, I can take it.

(OSWIN begins to beat him at first slowly, then harder and with more frequency, until ARNOLD begins to bleed, and OS-WIN shows disgust.)

OSWIN: That's enough. What do you think I am?. . .You sicken me, both of you. . .You are both poison to me! Let me go. . .
ARNOLD: Never! *(Holds him close) You are one of us. . .* Oswin, I need you. . .You must do a job for me. . .I am rich. . .I will pay you money. . .I mean I will be rich. I will pay you.
OSWIN: What are you talking about?
ARNOLD: You can guess. You know already. . .Kill him. Kill him.
OSWIN: *(Hypnotized, sick)* Kill who?
ARNOLD: You asshole. Who but him?
OSWIN: The Clown Master?
ARNOLD: Who else?
OSWIN: But I've given all that up! I'm clean!
ARNOLD: *(Seizes OSWIN and kisses him lengthily, holding on to him.)* You are mine, Oswin.

(OSWIN, sick, wipes his mouth.)

James Purdy

ARNOLD: You belong to us. . .Kill the Clown Master. Kill him.

OSWIN: *(Dreamy)* When? Yes?

ARNOLD: Killing is your thing. . .You are known as the perfect assassin. . .Why you never spent a night in jail even. You are perfect as Neil and I are perfect. . .But the Clown Master beshit you too as well as us. . .He tarred us. . .He ruined us. . . We are beggars! Beggars.

OSWIN: *(Brooding)* But the Clown Master loved Neil.

ARNOLD: Then why did he ruin us? Why are we beggars?

OSWIN: *(With passion)* I can't do it!

ARNOLD: Then you will have to die, Oswin.

OSWIN: Very well. Kill me. I'll not beg.

(ARNOLD seizes him, pushing him against the table. His bones crack.)

OSWIN: Neil, Neil! Save me! Save me.

(NEIL has collapsed, cannot move.)

ARNOLD: You've deserved death if only for coming here behind my back and making filthy love to my brother. Death is too good for you, crud that you are. . .

OSWIN: Wait. I'll do it.

ARNOLD: You're sure.

OSWIN: Let me up, you cheap. . .

ARNOLD: Watch your mouth. *(Puts his hand over OSWIN's lips.)*

OSWIN: I said I'd do it.

ARNOLD: When?

OSWIN: Whenever you like. Whenever I can get my hands on him.

ARNOLD: *(Rapt)* The Clown Master must die.

OSWIN: *(Falling into ARNOLD's mania)* All right. All right.

NEIL: *(Coming forward)* No, no. . .I forbid it. I will not be party to it.

10

ARNOLD: Go back to that bed and lie down.
NEIL: *(on his knees before* ARNOLD*)* By all that you hold dear, don't don't! *(And as he goes on kneeling before* ARNOLD, OSWIN *begins touching* ARNOLD'S *arm.)*
OSWIN: What am I to be paid for this?
ARNOLD: Name your price?
OSWIN: I want it in writing, signed by both of you then.
NEIL: Never, never.
ARNOLD: You'll have it in writing, Oswin, sweetheart. You'll have your price.

*(*OSWIN *takes out a sheet of paper from his coat, together with a pencil. He signals* ARNOLD *to sit down.)*

OSWIN: *(Dictating)* "I am to be paid a fair price by Arnold and Neil on my accomplishing the task which they have assigned to me. I will name my fair and just price on the day my task is accomplished."
ARNOLD: *(Indifferent and contemptuous of the actual wording.)* Fair enough. *(Signs.)* Neil, come over here, if you know what's good for you. . .Get!

*(*NEIL *comes over with great difficulty to the table.)*

ARNOLD: Put your name down there. Go on. Do you want me to cuff the daylights out of you? Put your name. . .there.

*(*NEIL *signs, weeping.* ARNOLD *hands the paper to* OSWIN *with lordly indifference.)*

ARNOLD: There you are. . .Now go do your work. . .
NEIL: Don't let him Arnold. Don't let him go. . .
ARNOLD: *(To* NEIL*)* So it was true. The Clown Master loved you!
NEIL: Don't let this happen, Arnold. *(*OSWIN *is already moving toward the door.)* Please, oh please, Arnold.

James Purdy

(OSWIN exits.)

NEIL: Call him back, Arnold, don't let him go do that terrible thing. Think of hell! Think of hell.

(ARNOLD soothes him by rubbing his neck and hair.)

ARNOLD: The only hell there is, Neil, is here. *(Kisses the back of his neck, goes on smoothing his hair.)* We will rest better when the dog is butchered and lying in the alley in a pool of his own blood. . .We will feel good on that occasion. . .You know that. . .

CURTAIN

SCENE TWO

The same. It is late the next day. NEIL *sits in the same chair as before, but without his clown makeup. He is in deep dejection. He covers himself with a quilt, though it is not cold in the room, and shakes his head. There is a sudden knocking at the door again, and he puts his hand over his eyes.*

NEIL: *(Calling out)* No one is to home. This flat is vacant! *(Laughs morosely.)* So go away, whoever you are. Only the fiend will let you in.

ELGA: *(Calls from outside.)* Neil! Let me in. It's Elga.

NEIL: I am forbidden to admit a living soul. *(Laughs.)*

ELGA: Neil, do you hear me?. . .Let me in. . .I have something to say to you. Be a good boy.

NEIL: You can rap till Kingdom Come, I will not open the door. He will beat the tar out of me if I open. He will beat the tar out of me anyhow.

ELGA: Then open the door. . .

NEIL: I don't have my shirt on.

ELGA: I'll wait.

(NEIL goes to a little bureau, takes out a flamboyantly-colored shirt with gold buttons, puts it on and tucks it into his trousers. He folds the quilt and throws it over his left arm like a waiter does with a large napkin.)

NEIL: *(Flinging open the door almost violently)* Well, Elga, why don't you step in.

ELGA: You're alone, thank God. . .*(Looks about apprehensively)* Where is the Fiend?

NEIL: Who knows? *(He comes over to her, kisses her, and then sits down, partly unfolding the quilt.)*

ELGA: While we have time, before Arnold comes back. . . tell me the truth, Neil. . .I will pay you with money if you tell me. . .Or give you that silk Persian handkerchief you admired so in the shop window. . .

NEIL: *(Passionately)* No! No.

ELGA: Tell me the truth. . .Hasn't your brother put my husband Oswin up to something? Tell me now, Neil.

(NEIL closes his eyes convulsively.)

ELGA: You must tell me. . .Just yes or no. . .Remember how many gifts I've given you in times past. . .

NEIL: I do not know. I do not know. So shut up. . .Don't pick at me.

ELGA: You know everything your brother says, does, or thinks, how many times he swallows during the day, you can count the number of times he snores at night. You know him better than you know yourself! You are like one soul in two bodies. . .So tell me. . .At least tell me if my husband was here. . .

NEIL: *(Reluctant)* Well, yes. Oswin was here yesterday.

ELGA: I knew it! I knew it. Oh, dear God. After all he promised me. . .And what was said, Neil darling? What did the two of them discuss? *(She kisses his hair and smoothes his neck, and his head falls gently toward her breast. She kisses him again and again, proving that they have often been in this posture before.)*

NEIL: I make a point of not listening.

ELGA: I promised your mother I would look after you, Neil. . .And haven't I? Haven't I kept that promise?

NEIL: I guess so.

ELGA: You guess so! I watched over you all the time you were in the circus, you know that. . .and after you got fired. . . *(To herself)* But I will watch again once I am free of the baby. . . *(NEIL moves uneasily under her caresses.)* What do you want from the fancy clothes store, Neil?

NEIL: *(Breathless)* The jewel-studded necktie.

ELGA: You shall have it.

NEIL: When?

ELGA: As soon as you tell me what happened. . .we'll go to the store, and I will put it into your hands.

NEIL: But it costs a fortune.

ELGA: Then it costs a fortune. Nothing is too good for you darling. *(She kisses him with real passion.)*

NEIL: It must cost a whole year's labor.

ELGA: You'll tell me then?

NEIL: *(Pouting, uncooperative)* Tell you what I don't know?

ELGA: *(Slaps him)* You simpleton!

NEIL: *(Seizes her arm brutally so that he resembles ARNOLD.)* Don't you ever call me that again, you whore, or you'll regret it. . .And now I'll tell you nothing. Keep your damned old jeweled necktie. . .Arnold will buy it for me!

ELGA: *Arnold!* Hear him. Arnold wouldn't buy you clothes to bury you in!

NEIL: *(Frightened)* What a queer thing to say.

ELGA: Well, forgive me. . .At any rate we all know how tight Arnold is. He has money stashed away somewhere too. He was big there in the circus until he went crazy.

NEIL: *(Hard)* I have no information for you.

ELGA: Oh yes you do!. . .Now see here, you little snot. . .I have some things on you, too. . .If you know what's good for you, you'll talk. . .What did Arnold tell Oswin to do? Answer me!

NEIL: *(Hardening still more)* I didn't listen to them.

ELGA: *(Frantic)* But they were talking a lot, weren't they—like they were plotting?

NEIL: *(Memory forcing him out, crying)* Yes. . .yes!. . . They were plotting. . .

ELGA: You shall have the necktie, darling.

NEIL: *(Remembering, talking as if in his sleep)* I begged him not to. . .

ELGA: Yes, yes. . .

NEIL: I begged him not to ask him to kill him.

ELGA: Kill who, sweetheart?

NEIL: *(Cries hard, and* ELGA *comforts him lavishly)* Who but the Clown Master?

ELGA: *(Horrified in spite of herself)* Oh God, and with me in this condition. . .

NEIL: I begged Arnold not to force him to do so.

ELGA: Of course you did! *(Thinking it over)* So Arnold told Oswin he must kill the Clown Master? *(She speaks comfortingly, soothingly, siren-like, making* NEIL *think he has said something everybody knows.)*

NEIL: But, wait. . .I never said that to you. . .I never told you!

ELGA: But I knew it already!

NEIL: Did Oswin tell you?

ELGA: I just knew it.

NEIL: You lie! You wormed it out of me. . .And now Arnold will mangle me! *(Weeps)* He will kill me. . .

ELGA: He shan't touch you, dearest darling boy. . .Not one hair of your head!

NEIL: A big help you would be! When I'm here all the time unprotected!

(ELGA grimaces suddenly in pain, and lets out a scream.)

NEIL: What is it?

ELGA: The baby. . .I'm five months gone. . .He moves so rough. . .Neil, I do not want to have this baby. . .I don't want it. *(To herself)* I won't have it.

NEIL: No?

16

ELGA: *(Craftily)* By the way. . .A long time ago, well, I know your mother gave some of our friends a kind of medicine when they didn't want to have a baby. . .

NEIL: *(Mooning)* That's so. . .

ELGA: You wouldn't by chance still have any somewhere?

NEIL: I might. . .But you must promise never to tell Arnold. And never tell him I told you about Oswin and he plotting.

ELGA: I will never tell anybody if you will only give me the medicine.

NEIL: But the medicine is very strong, Elga.

ELGA: I must not have this baby!

NEIL: But it's dangerous! Some women die when they take it. . .I warn you.

ELGA: Listen, listen carefully. . .Neil, darling. This baby is by your brother.

NEIL: *(In horror)* No! No! No! *(Offers to hit her.)*

ELGA: What is it, Neil? Aren't we friends? Don't I love you even more than Arnold does or your mother did?

NEIL: *(Sobs)* He told me. . .I was his baby. . .

ELGA: *(Frightened)* What are you talking about? *(Shakes him.)*

NEIL: *(Incoherent)* I am Arnold's only love.

ELGA: *(Gaining control over herself)* Of course you are, Neil. . .What is a woman's love compared to how he loves you. . .You are Arnold's whole life. . .

NEIL: *(Appeased)* I know that, Elga.

ELGA: But see here. I cannot have Arnold's baby. . .Oswin is sterile and he knows it. And he hasn't noticed yet I am pregnant. . .Thinks I'm putting on weight. I must have that medicine.

NEIL: *(Drowsily)* You'll buy me then the jeweled necktie?

ELGA: Didn't I say I would.

NEIL: *(Moody, angry)* So he is the father.

ELGA: As I said.

NEIL: Well, then. . .You know the little medicine chest in the bathroom, Elga. . .The medicine is in the second drawer from the

17

top. There are two boxes in the drawer. One is pink colored, the other is dark blue. Tiny hard yellow pills. Take the whole box. Chew one pill every two hours until. . .

(ELGA has already gone out of the room, out of earshot.)

NEIL: . . .until you're cemetary-bound. . .how could he love her, and love me? I am his love. . .I am his only love. . .Death is too good for her. . .

ELGA: *(Re-entering)* Thank you, Neil.

NEIL: *(In a sudden panic)* Don't take those pills, Elga! Please! They can cause you great harm.

ELGA: No, you're mistaken. I remember the pills when Daphne took them—. They gave her a miscarriage.

NEIL: But she died later on!

ELGA: Ah, but that was from something else. . .Months, months later she died of a heart attack.

NEIL: Don't swallow them. . .here, give them back to me. . . They're poison. . .I lied to you. . .I'm jealous of Arnold!

ELGA: No, no. I want the pills. . .I won't have this baby! I won't. Shut up. . .Do you want your jeweled necktie or not!

NEIL: *(Weeps passionately)* Give me the pills, Elga. . . They're rank poison. . .

ELGA: I'll go buy your necktie now and see it's sent to you.

NEIL: Elga! Elga! Don't swallow them. . .I've lied to you! They're poison.

ELGA: Goodbye. . .Remember, we keep each other's secrets. . .*(Suddenly stops, as if she had a premonition.)* Remember, Neil, the day you lay naked with me all afternoon.

NEIL: Yes, but that was long ago. I am not the father.

ELGA: You were beautiful. But he should not have a son. . . You are his love, Neil. . .

NEIL: Of course.

ELGA: It's too bad the Clown Master must die.

NEIL: Ah, yes. . .

ELGA: But the main thing is that Oswin must not know I am pregnant. . .Anyhow I hated the Clown Master.

(NEIL shades his face, ELGA goes out. He is by now only half aware she has come and gone.)

NEIL: Oh, my God. Elga will die. But I warned her. I told her, but not clearly enough. . .Yet Arnold had no right to be the father! He belongs to me. . .I am his child. . .He had no right. . .She will die. The Clown Master will die. . .Oh, help! Mother! Mother! Oh, Mother, protect your son. . .My God, my God. . .

CURTAIN

SCENE THREE

*ELGA is discovered in her home drinking a glass of water
thirstily, slowly, with difficulty. The pill box which NEIL has
given her is held in her left hand.
The house in which she lives with her husband OSWIN is full of
light in contrast with ARNOLD and NEIL's flat, and soft, as if
it were made of the plumage of white birds. A great bed is in the
rear of the room stacked with pillows, a bed such as a Queen or
rich invalid might possess.*

ELGA: *(Swallowing again and again)* What has he given me?
(Looks at the pill box, smells inside.) What have I taken?. . .It
doesn't taste a thing like his mother's remedy. . .No, it's not the
same medicine I took before. . .But why would Neil want to kill
me. *(OSWIN has entered but is too distraught to notice the state
his wife is in, and stands hollow-eyed and bent.)* I don't care what
I've swallowed. . .I've lived too long already.
OSWIN: *(Closing the door)* What are you raving about now?
ELGA: Why don't you knock when you come into my room?
OSWIN: You have no room. I own everything you touch.
(About to run away, he sees the box of medicine.) What's this?
ELGA: What do you suppose it is?
OSWIN: Where did you get this suspicious stuff?
ELGA: Where do you suppose?
OSWIN: You will address your husband properly. Answer my
question! *(He takes the box of medicine from her in a fury, sniffs
in it.)* Did you hear what I said?
ELGA: I've never heard you for I've never loved you.

OSWIN: But you married me.

ELGA: My worst mistake.

OSWIN: *(Tasting the medicine cautiously)* Look here, who gave you this stuff, Elga! *(Crumbles the pills in his hand, and spits on the floor what he has tasted.)* This is a dangerous thing. . .Have you taken it?

ELGA: The apothecary gave it to me.

OSWIN: What apothecary?

ELGA: *(Feeling the power of the medicine)* Help me to the bed, Oswin.

(He assists her to lie down in the bed, loosens her clothing, etc.)

OSWIN: *(Bending over her)* My poor girl. You are the color of paste.

ELGA: He knew I didn't want to live.

OSWIN: Who?

ELGA: Oswin, I am pregnant.

OSWIN: *(His mind far off)* I hope it's by the Clown Master.

ELGA: *(Suspicious, comes awake)* Oswin, what are you up to? I knew when I saw you come in you had returned to your old life!

OSWIN: Not so, Elga. . .I have not had my hands in blood for a year. . .But tell me the Clown Master has abused you. . .Make me hate him. . .hard. Fill me wth murder for one last time, Elga, then I will be your man. You can be a whore all you like. Have other men five, twenty times a day, but be mine. Hold me at night from my dreams! Elga, I love you. . .almost best.

ELGA: You love Neil. He is your love, and it is *him* who gave me this poison.

OSWIN: Then I'll murder him too.

ELGA: *(Sleepily)* Murder the only being you ever loved?. . . *(Almost inaudible)* I am quoting now. I am quoting. *(Begins to spit up something.)* Oh, God. . .Oswin. Call the doctor.

OSWIN: You said. . .you mean Neil would want you to

die?. . .*(To himself)* That must mean he is willing to run off with me. . .

ELGA: Go for help, Oswin. . .Go for someone. . .I am in terrible pain.

OSWIN: *(Leisurely)* I'll fix an antidote. . .This is not a bad poison. *(Goes out of the room.)*

ELGA: No, I want to die. I don't want to be old and unwanted. Now all of them want me, the Clown Master, Arnold, Neil, even Oswin. All, alldesire me as they desire one another. I am their Divine Mother. Let me die perfect. Let me hold them beyond the grave.

OSWIN: *(Returning with a tumbler)* Drink this, dearest one.

ELGA: I don't need it.

OSWIN: I say drink it.

ELGA: It's too late, Oswin.

OSWIN: Give me your blessing for my last job.

ELGA: My thoughts are so every-which-way. What do you have to do to be blessed for?

OSWIN: Listen. Can you hear me? I have promised Arnold I will kill the Clown Master for a price which he has agreed to without knowing what it is. Understand?

ELGA: Of course. A bargain. *(She is dying.)*

OSWIN: I ask you, Elga, to give me your blessing since you hint that the Clown Master has wronged you by giving you this baby. . .

ELGA: *(Bitter)* Someone has.

OSWIN: Someone? Elga! Tell me I may kill the Clown Master. Give me your blessing. Impart to me your strength! Elga, I love you. You are as you always say my Divine Mother.

ELGA: What is your price? What must Arnold give you?

OSWIN: Neil.

ELGA: He will never surrender his only love and care to you.

OSWIN: Ah, but I have it written down here. Signed by both Neil and Arnold!

ELGA: Let me see their hands.

OSWIN: Here, here. *(Shows her the paper.)*

James Purdy

ELGA: The brothers. The brothers' hands. I loved them. I loved the Clown Master. I loved you all. I am the. . .One. *(The pain takes possession of her, she struggles with death.)*
OSWIN: Elga, Elga. . .Your blessing. Give it. *(Kisses her feet. She lifts herself up and smoothes his head.)*
ELGA: If you must return to your old life then, what better assignment than to kill the Clown Master. . .Kill him, Oswin. . .
OSWIN: Thank you, Elga, thank you. God thank you forever. . .*(Stares at her in terror.)* Are you better?
ELGA: Much better. . .But, Oswin. . .
OSWIN: Yes, my dearest girl. . .
ELGA: Cut out his tongue when you've killed him. . .
OSWIN: *(As if struck deaf)* What? Who?
ELGA: Cut out the Clown Master's tongue—to the root.
OSWIN: Yes. . .But why?
ELGA: He killed my brother, and it was him who gave me lust before I was ready for love. . .Years ago. . .he took me. . .with promises first from his lying organ of speech. . .Cut it off. . .Furthermore. . .you need proof that he is dead to show to Arnold. . . Once he has seen the Clown Master's tongue he will bestow Neil on you.
OSWIN: *(Sick)* I don't want to do it.
ELGA: *(Coming up for a moment as from deep water)* What don't you want?
OSWIN: The tongue! How horrible! If I did such a thing, how could I take Neil?
ELGA: Have you lost your character?
OSWIN: I don't know.
ELGA: Then take one of the remaining pills in the box. Join me.
OSWIN: I love Neil.
ELGA: How long have you loved him?
OSWIN: Since the day I set eyes on him in the circus when I visited the dressing room, when I saw his pink flesh. . .
ELGA: Then why do you hesitate to kill the Clown Master?
OSWIN: What sort of fiend are you! To talk of cutting off

24

tongues! You whore!
ELGA: You flinch only because it is what you wish to do. . .
What we wish to do is always horrible to us. . .And if you don't
kill the Clown Master, you may be sure he will kill you. . .
OSWIN: How do you know this?

(*ELGA dies, falls into his arms.*)

OSWIN: Elga! Elga!. . .(*Lets her fall to the bed.*) Ah, Neil,
Neil. . .So this is what it means. . .You have freed me from her
for you!. . .But the tongue! The tongue. Yet she has commanded
it. . .A dead woman has commanded I am to cut off his tongue. I
will run mad down the street. . .Why is it so afflicting. . .Look at
my hands! (*He holds his hands up close to his eyes, and lets out
great cries.*)

CURTAIN

SCENE FOUR

The house of the CLOWN MASTER.
It is severely furnished in its richness, as the Clown Brothers' in their poverty. A great gold chair sits in the middle of the stage, and two smaller chairs at the left of it. An immense chandelier hangs from the ceiling directly over the chair. Many candelabra are burning in memory of ELGA, *whom the* CLOWN MASTER *believes he once loved.*
Enter CLYDE, *a servant, who dusts everything rapidly, polishes the lion claw feet of the great chair, arranges the chair's cushions, etc.*
The CLOWN MASTER *enters. He is taller than* ARNOLD, *but not so massive looking, but an obvious prince of power and anomalous wickedness—in this perhaps surpassing* ARNOLD.

CLOWN MASTER: Clyde, we are to have a visitor this morning. . .A widower. Fresh from the graveside he's coming.
CLYDE: Yes, sir.
CLOWN MASTER: Do you have your notebook and sharpened pencils—the kind with the very soft lead which will make no sound?
CLYDE: I do, sir.
CLOWN MASTER: Let me see your fingers.

(CLYDE *stretches out his hands.*)

CLOWN MASTER: Aha, pretty steady. . .You have not been drinking? Or smoking stuff?

CLYDE: I have touched none of those things since I came into service here, sir. You know that. . .

CLOWN MASTER: *(Coming close to* CLYDE, *as if to kiss him)* Never touch anything stronger while you remain here with me—than my own breath! Is that clear? Or you know what will happen otherwise. . .

CLYDE: My only wish in this life is to serve you. . .You saved me from my old life. . .

CLOWN MASTER: *(Interrupting contemptuously)* Then listen close. . .Elga has been murdered—I think by Arnold, the First Clown in the circus of some time past. . .As long as Arnold lives, we are not safe. . .Do you hear?

(He sits in the big chair. CLYDE *stands mute with head bowed.)*

CLOWN MASTER: When the widower, Oswin, comes today, do not miss a syllable of what he says, and make no noise. He must not think he is overheard. . .Fetch out that screen.

(CLYDE hurriedly brings out a huge screen which is so heavy and cumbersome that the CLOWN MASTER *rises to help him put it in place.)*

CLOWN MASTER: Good boy. You will stand behind it. He will be here at any minute. Best take off your shoes. *(CLYDE removes his shoes.)* And your socks also. *(Muses as* CLYDE *stands in bare feet.)* Why didn't you tell me you had such beautiful feet, Clyde?

CLYDE: You never asked me to show them to you. *(Almost forgetting, adds)* Sir.

CLOWN MASTER: *(Dreamy)* Your feet are more beautiful than those of any woman's. . .How does this come about?

(There is a sound of a bell ringing.)

CLOWN MASTER: *(Coming out of his reverie)* That's him.

(CLYDE picks up his shoes and socks and goes behind the screen. The CLOWN MASTER *waits until he is sure* CLYDE *has become settled in his place as eavesdropper, then goes to admit the visitor.* OSWIN *enters.)*

CLOWN MASTER: Why are you not dressed in black?
OSWIN: *(Sarcastic)* Why does His Majesty open his door with his own hands?
CLOWN MASTER: Ah.

(OSWIN looks about suspiciously.)

CLOWN MASTER: Will you have something to drink?
OSWIN: I will drink whatever you are drinking.

(CLOWN MASTER goes to a little table, pours a cordial into two small glasses, hands OSWIN *one, then takes up the other.)*

CLOWN MASTER: Let us drink to the memory of Elga.
OSWIN: No, Clown Master. I cannot do that.
CLOWN MASTER: Then let us drink to our old and present friendship.
OSWIN: Very well. Why not?

(They drink.)

CLOWN MASTER: Be seated, Oswin. You are at home here.

(OSWIN goes on standing, looking around him with growing uneasiness.)

OSWIN: I prefer to sit over yonder. *(Points to a chair the furthest from the screen but facing it.)*

James Purdy

CLOWN MASTER: That is not a comfortable chair, I'm afraid.

OSWIN: Comfort is the last thing on my mind.

CLOWN MASTER: Under the circumstances, how could it be otherwise?

OSWIN: Come to the point. Why have you summoned me, almost from the graveside of my wife. What is your wish. . .Be quick.

CLOWN MASTER: I am surprised at your haste. I never knew you to be in a hurry before.

OSWIN: I want to be locked up with my grief. Each word heard from others or pronounced by myself is pain.

CLOWN MASTER: I believe you mean that. . .I believe you loved Elga.

OSWIN: No, I did not love her. . .But I needed her. She killed herself. . .She did not want to have her baby. . .The doctor has told me everything. We buried her nonetheless without scandal. . .

CLOWN MASTER: Who was the father of her baby?

OSWIN: As if you don't know!

CLOWN MASTER: Oswin, watch your tongue.

OSWIN: *(At the word* tongue, *he becomes upset and moans.)* What? What! What.

CLOWN MASTER: *(Rushing to the table for the cordial and pouring* OSWIN *another glass.)* Drink this off at once.

(OSWIN, after coughing violently, downs the second glass.)

CLOWN MASTER: I have never seen you so overwrought. . .Stay seated. . .Be steady. . .We will not talk today.

OSWIN: No, no. . .I am all right now. Clown Master, I do not like to come here, you know that. . .You always remind me of how far down. . .on the scale I have remained. . .Tell me what it is you require of me so I may go. . .I am not at ease I say in your house! I am afraid here. . .Why not say it!

CLOWN MASTER: You, a hired assassin, afraid of me! What a compliment. . .

30

OSWIN: I am no longer that, Clown Master! I am clean. My hands have been washed free of blood for a long time. I will never go back to that again. . .If only in memory of Elga. . .

CLOWN MASTER: . . .who was murdered!

OSWIN: Ah, ah. . .

CLOWN MASTER: By order of Arnold!

OSWIN: *(Struck by the idea.)* You think so?

CLOWN MASTER: *(Nods.)* And you will be next!

OSWIN: I?. . .I. . .*(He begins to laugh in a maniacal way.)*

CLOWN MASTER: *(Alarmed)* Never laugh that way again in my presence!. . .Do you hear?

OSWIN: *(Menacingly subservient)* Yes, Clown Master.

CLOWN MASTER: *(Leans over from his chair)* I think if I heard that laugh repeatedly I would run crazy!

OSWIN: You don't mean that. . .You are too strong. . .

CLOWN MASTER: Where did you inherit such a terrible laugh! Jesus Christ Almighty! *(Shudders with horror)* It's not human. . .

OSWIN: *(Beginning to remember his mission)* You would not like to hear it late at night after you've been some time asleep then?

CLOWN MASTER: *(Stares at him wonderingly)* We were` saying, then Oswin. . .It is dangerous for both of us to allow Arnold to live. . .

OSWIN: He has never killed anybody in the past.

CLOWN MASTER: He killed Elga.

OSWIN: No, she stole some poison from little Neil. He has told me all. . .

CLOWN MASTER: *(Tenderly)* Little Neil. . .How is he?

OSWIN: He is pining away. . .

CLOWN MASTER: That is why we must get rid of Arnold. . .He is not a fit person to bring up the boy. Neil belongs with me. . .*(Almost to himself)* But he must never be a Clown again. . .

OSWIN: *(To himself)* We will see who Neil belongs with. *(His attention is occupied again with the screen. He looks under the base of it, sees the naked feet of CLYDE.)*

31

James Purdy

CLOWN MASTER: *(Lost in thought, is not watching* OSWIN*)* You must go back into harness, Oswin. . .You must kill Arnold.

OSWIN: What? *(Said more in horror of there being someone behind the screen, than the offer to be an assassin of* NEIL's *brother.)*

CLOWN MASTER: So name your price.

OSWIN: *(Covers his eyes with his palms.)* My price! My price. . .I tell you I have retired.

CLOWN MASTER: A great assassin canot retire. And you are great. Look at your hands. *(He has risen and takes* OSWIN's *hands down from his eyes and spreads them out.)* Beautiful as those of the greatest violinist or sculptor. . .But meant to strike down. They are the hands which bestow death. . .Perfectly, Oswin. . .Perfectly. . .I love you.

OSWIN: Spare me, Clown Master. Release me. Release me, let me go! *(Screams.)* Who is behind the screen there? Who is it? Is it Arnold? *(Rushes over and pulls down the screen, revealing* CLYDE, *who lets out great cries and rushes out of the room.)* Oh, oh. I thought it was Arnold behind the screen. I did, I did. . .

CLOWN MASTER: *(Goes over to him, soothes him with his hand.)* Be calm. Trust me.

*(*OSWIN *laughs his maniacal laugh, and the* CLOWN MASTER *stops his ears, shuddering.)*

CLOWN MASTER: *(Slowly recovering himself)* You must do me this favor, Oswin. . .It is a little favor to ask in light of what you have done before. Just one more killing, and you are free! Just Arnold. *(The* CLOWN MASTER *kisses him on the face, and* OSWIN *draws away barely restraining himself from wiping the kiss off.)* You are perfect, Oswin. Do it for me. . .And now name your price.

OSWIN: You name it for me. My brain is not clear.

CLOWN MASTER: Is twenty-five thousand dollars enough?

OSWIN: No.

32

CLOWN MASTER: *(Shocked)* Well, say thirty thousand.
OSWIN: Impossible.
CLOWN MASTER: Forty then?
OSWIN: *(Infuriated)* Never!
CLOWN MASTER: Name your price then, you niggling cruddy bandit! *(Slaps him viciously.)*
OSWIN: *(Wiping off the blood contemptuously)* All right. I'll name *him*.

(CLOWN MASTER, frightened in spite of himself, draws back.)

OSWIN: My price is Neil.
CLOWN MASTER: *(Dissembling, plotting)* Very well, then, fifty thousand and the boy.
OSWIN: *(Icy)* Agreed, Clown Master. . .Agreed.
CLOWN MASTER: And when will you accomplish it?
OSWIN: This very night. . .
CLOWN MASTER: *(Deeply moved in spite of himself)* Before you go, Oswin, let me give you a down payment. . .It is not right you should go without an advance. . .

(As the CLOWN MASTER turns his back on OSWIN and moves toward a partition in the wall which opens under his pressure, OSWIN carefully unsheathes a knife, creeps up slowly to the CLOWN MASTER.)

OSWIN: Open up a circus in hell! *(Stabs him again and again. . .The CLOWN MASTER falls to the floor without uttering a word, dead. . .OSWIN bends over his body.)*

(CLYDE enters.)

CLYDE: What was that noise? What has happened?
OSWIN: The Clown Master has killed himself.
CLYDE: Killed himself? In the back?

OSWIN: Yes, he fell on his own knife, see? It's easy to do when one is careless.

CLYDE: What in God's name are you doing to his mouth!

OSWIN: I am cutting out his tongue! To the root! *(He rises with the bleeding tongue in his hand.)* See, see it. . .Behold, it will never command you again. *(Stabs* CLYDE *again and again with his free hand. The servant falls over the body of his Master.)* See your Master's tongue, you filthy eavesdropper. Why does it not command you? Why is it so quiet and still? *(Kicks the body of* CLYDE.*)*

CURTAIN

SCENE FIVE

ARNOLD'S *flat.*
NEIL *is welcoming* OSWIN *as the scene commences.*
NEIL *holds a toy piano in his left hand. They bow to one another like characters in a shadow-play.* NEIL *comes forward almost to the footlights and looks out into space. He shakes his head. Then he comes to one of the chairs and sits down. He plays a few notes on the toy piano.*
OSWIN *has not yet fully entered the room. He is only hours from having murdered the* CLOWN MASTER *and* CLYDE. *He is dazed, nearly immobile. He holds a leather pouch. Then he comes rapidly forward and stands behind* NEIL'S *chair. He stretches his hand out to touch* NEIL, *then he thinks better of it, and withdraws it. His head is bowed again.*
NEIL *plays some more on the little piano.*

OSWIN: I didn't know you knew music.

NEIL: I didn't until Arnold brought me this little paino. He found it lying outside a wealthy person's mansion.

OSWIN: *(Gasping)* Neil, I have come to claim you.

(NEIL *puts down the piano and covers his eyes with the palm of his right hand.*)

OSWIN: You are mine now. *(To himself.)* I have earned you.

(NEIL *picks up the piano and plays a few notes.*)

OSWIN: Mine, mine forever and a day. . .Do you know how I loved you. . .Of course you do not. . .I love you like all the statues of baby Jesus in all the churches of the world. I will worship you throughout life and bring you all you need. I worship you now. . .I have fulfilled my promise. . .Let us go.

NEIL: *(Somberly)* Very well, Oswin. . .Shall I bring the piano?

OSWIN: Do you need it?

NEIL: *(Looking at it in his outstretched hand)* Since it was from Arnold, and I am to go with you, perhaps not.

OSWIN: Oh, take it along, why don't you. You play besides so nice. *(He wishes to touch NEIL, but is afraid to,. and keeps hugging the leather pouch inside his coat.)* Where is Arnold?

NEIL: *(Dazed)* Isn't he here?

(OSWIN stares at NEIL.)

NEIL: *(Rubs his eyes)* Well, he must have just gone out for something. . .He often steals out, steals in. . .

OSWIN: *(Looks about apprehensively)* Perhaps he's in the back somewhere.

NEIL: *(Firmly)* No. . .Oswin, what is it? Are you ill?

OSWIN: Yes! Oh, yes.

NEIL: *(Coldly)* Where do you feel bad? *(He rises and draws near him.)*

OSWIN: Don't touch me. . .I did it all for you, Neil.

NEIL: *(Frightened)* What. . .all for me?

OSWIN: You have forgotten already? *(Dreamily)* I have killed the Clown Master for you.

NEIL: *(Calm, glacial)* Oh.

OSWIN: Is that all you have to say—*oh!*

NEIL: I forbade you to do it but you obeyed Arnold.

OSWIN: Then why didn't you stop me? Why didn't you stand in the way!

NEIL: Because at that time. . .I was not yet free.

(NEIL's eyes rove to the back of the room over the wall of which is now stretched a huge quilt. OSWIN *looks at the stretched quilt with indifference, then he looks at it again, first with wonder and perplexity, then with awe and horror.)*

OSWIN: You say at that time?. . .

(NEIL goes over to a little stand where his makeup box rests, begins slowly to put on his Clown face.)

OSWIN: *(Shakes his head, rubs his eyes.)* You said you were going away with me. *(NEIL goes on preparing himsef to be a Clown.)* Neil! Neil! Or are you Neil. . .*(With terror)*Are you him?. . .Are *you* Arnold? *(He looks over at the quilt)* Tell me, for God's sake. You don't know what I've been through. . .Look here. (He picks up the leather pouch, points to it.)

NEIL: What is this? *(He now resembles* ARNOLD *so much that* OSWIN *hardly dares to look at him.)* Part of your dis-obedience!

OSWIN: Oh, Neil, Neil. . .I have never loved you more!

NEIL: What is in this blood-soaked pouch?

OSWIN: *(With terrible effort)* It is. . .the tongue. . .of the Clown Master.

NEIL: *(Draws back.)* By command of who?

OSWIN: By command of her.

NEIL: Her? Who?

OSWIN: The whore in my life.

NEIL: Why should she want his tongue. . .cut.

OSWIN: *(Finishing the sentence for him)* To the. . .root. . .

NEIL: *(In a kind of trance)* Ah, then that is something I have forgotten, Oswin. It slipped my mind. Or did I know? Did Elga tell me also? No, she forgot. . .

OSWIN: Neil, take off your Clown makeup. . .I do not love you as a Clown. You look too much like Arnold!

NEIL: Oswin, you speak too much like he did!. . .Have a care. . .You must not anger me also! You must not command me

37

now!. . .I will never again be commanded, do you hear?

OSWIN: But how can I love you, hold you to me if you look like a Clown, if you look like him!

NEIL: Ah. . .But I want to be a Clown. . .

OSWIN: More than you want to be mine?

NEIL: I want to be yours, yes. . .But I am a Clown. . .I am the last Clown now.

(OSWIN begins to understand and is tempted to look at the outstretched quilt, but resists the impulse.)

NEIL: *(Almost weeping)* There is now only you and I, Oswin, only you and I, my dear friend. Embrace me! Embrace me. . . Don't mind the paint. . .

OSWIN: My dearest boy. . .It is you only I have loved all these years. . .I will give up all my past ways if you will only leave with me now. . .And if you must wear the Clown paint, very well, very well. . .

NEIL: But how could I have forgotten the last touch? The last little thing in the performance, Oswin.

(He picks up the toy piano dispiritedly, he plays a few notes on it. OSWIN shudders, looks again at the quilt, and then down at the floor. NEIL again in a sort of trance, drops the little piano, which breaks and falls to pieces.)

NEIL: Arnold, who was a great performer, my dear brother, always said, *In every great performance, there is one last touch, without which something would be lacking.* . .You see I had forgotten it, and you have brought it to my mind. . .Thank you also for killing the Clown Master.

(OSWIN turns away from him in horror.)

NEIL: We were, after all, one. That is why Arnold should never have deceived me all these years. . .He lied to me!. . .Arnold lied!. . .He had promised that I would always be allowed to join him should there ever again be a Clown act beyond the *purlieus* of the Circus. . .Yes, those were his words. . .Beyond the purlieus. . .But at the last, you see. . .he received this other appointment. . .He said he was tired of being a beggar. . .This other appointment did not include me. . .*You must remain here, Neil*, he said, *until I can send for you. I will have to be the Clown from now on for both of us.* And then, Oswin, do you know what he said.

(OSWIN *has buried his head in his arms like one who would be deaf and blind.*)

NEIL: He said, *Neil, darling boy, I love you more than life, but you were never meant to be a Clown. . .You are only a little boy whom I love more than life. . .You were never considered a real Clown. Don't you see? They only permitted you to play Clown because of me, because I am the great Clown, Neil. . .The greatest perhaps who ever lived. . .And so I must go out now and make my name for both of us. . .You are my life, Neil, my only love. . .But you are not a Clown.*

(OSWIN *moans, still holding his ears.*)

NEIL: *Take back what you've just said, Arnold*, I told him. *You have lied to me, but you can still take back your words. Take them back, for otherwise you have lied to me all your life, and I have lived only on your lies. For you told me I was a Clown, and we will be Clowns and Brothers forever. . .*But Arnold said, *You are my life, my heart, my all, but I am the only Clown. . .I would give you my life, but I cannot admit you to my fellowship, for I am the only Clown.*

(*He goes to* OSWIN, *and touches him, and* OSWIN *shudders as if touched by a hot iron.*)

NEIL: *Then, Arnold,* I said, *you must die. . .For I am the Greater Clown, and the Circus Clown Master knew it. . .I am the Greater. . .*

(He rushes to the quilt stretched over the back wall, rips it down, revealing ARNOLD, *nearly naked, hanging dead from two hooks, his head fallen down.)*

OSWIN: *(Looks up)* Oh God, Jesus Almighty!. . .Help me, Help me. . .

NEIL: *(Apostrophizing the dead* ARNOLD*)* I am the Greater Clown! Arnold, admit it. I am the Greater. . .But, wait, wait, the last touch, oh Elga, thank you, thank you, Divine Mother. . .*(He takes his brother's head in his hands, and then taking a knife from his pocket, he cuts out* ARNOLD'S *tongue, and then advancing, holds it up to a horrified* OSWIN.*)* Here, here, cut to the root, is that lying organ. . .Oswin, before you take me away with you, shall we not eat it, shall we not eat his tongue, you and I together. . .Say yes, Oswin. . .Say we shall partake of his lying tongue. *(After a silence he proffers the tongue to* OSWIN, *who recoils and falls on his knees.)*

OSWIN: Kill me, Neil. . .Neil, Neil. . .Kill me. . .Neil, have pity on me. . .You are strong and young. . .See, my arms have lost their strength. . .I have lost my profession. . .See, Neil. . . Kill me. . .Kill me. . .Kill me. . .

CURTAIN

TRUE

True, by James Purdy, had its world premiere, in New York City on June 30, 1978 at the Westbeth Theatre Centre. The play was given a second performance on July 1, 1978. *True* was directed by Duane Mazey, and the part of Chester was played by Edward Gierke. John Uecker played Ewen. Chester's age was changed in the Westbeth production to that of a boy of twenty as it was found too difficult even for an experienced actor to portray a thirteen year old boy.

CHESTER: I've never lied to you, Ewen, never.

EWEN: Oh, you've lied to me from time to time ever since you could talk. Not real lies, little made-up things. But today you see you lied. You lied big to me today. *(He mumbles and shakes his head.)* So as a result I may have to give you away.

CHESTER: Give me away? Why, isn't that what you'd call a threat?

EWEN: I don't need to threaten you. . .You threaten yourself when you talk the way you've been talking. *(Drowsily)* You see you scare yourself.

CHESTER: All of a sudden you are mean to me, after all the years you were good to me. Suddenly you give me the shitty end of the stick.

EWEN: *(slapping him)* Don't ever let me hear you use such words. I brought you up better than that.

CHESTER: *(whimpering)* You see, you have changed. Threats, slaps.

EWEN: Calm down now. . .There, there. *(He holds him gently on his lap.)* You musn't make yourself sick now. . .Now now.

CHESTER: Tell me how I lied to you.

EWEN: It don't matter. You're my brother and it don't matter.

CHESTER: I want to be true.

EWEN: Just rest in my arms, why don't you? See, get quiet. . . That's right. When you get riled you don't feel so good. . .It don't matter anyhow about your thinking you lied or if I said you lied. . . It don't matter. You can lie to me or you can tell me the truth. I am your brother.

CHESTER: But I didn't lie, Ewen. Or imagine. I saw him kill the boy.

EWEN: Oh, here we go again. Oh, oh.

CHESTER: I swear to you, Ewen. I swear by. . .by *(looking out)* the church spire.

EWEN: And you just watched him kill him, you didn't try to stop it. . .

CHESTER: Him? Oh. . .what could I do, Ewen. . .He raised the knife before I could get ready to scream. . .The man who saw the knife raised over him started to cry out, at last he opened his mouth wide, but the knife plunged downwards, down, down. *(He cries and hides his head in his brother's shirt.)* Oh, oh, oh.

EWEN: Chester, Chester. . .See here, you imagined it. . .See here. *(He slaps him.)* Wake up!

CHESTER: Don't hit me for telling the truth now. . .Don't.

EWEN: All right. . .He stabbed him then. You saw it. . .Why did you wait so long then to tell me. . .Why?

CHESTER: A day—is that long?

EWEN: Yes, it's long. . .*(Quickly)* Chester, you lied.

CHESTER: No, no, I told the truth. . .Ewen, my hand—you hold it too tight.

EWEN: You lie. There was no murder.

CHESTER: Did I call it a murder?

EWEN: You said he raised a knife and killed him.

CHESTER: Is that murder?

EWEN: Well, it ain't givin birth to a baby is it?

CHESTER: *(dreamy)* I wish I had not seen it. . .Ewen, what are you thinking about.

EWEN: I'm tired of you burdening me with your lies.

CHESTER: You shouldn't ever be tired of me. . .I'll quit lying then.

EWEN: Then you admit it was a lie, do you. Damn it all.

CHESTER: Oh, no, no. It was true, but if it makes you feel better I'll say it was a lie. For you, you see, I'll say any—

EWEN: Oh, God Almighty. Stand up. . .Go on, stand up, Chester. *(Chester stands up. He is very small and stunted in growth for a boy of thirteen.)* Now, answer me truthful, tell me the very rock-bottom truth. . .Did you see another man stab a man.

CHESTER: No.

EWEN: You lied to me then.

CHESTER: I'm telling you I didn't see him do it to make you feel better, Ewen. No, I saw nothing. No stabbing.

EWEN: Oh, God. My God. I think I'm going crazy. . .Now see here. . .Did you see it, and if so, where. . .Where did it take place. . .?

CHESTER: *(whispering into his brother's ear)* In the back room of Hattie's saloon.

EWEN: What in the hell were you doing in there, you're no more than a child, huh.

CHESTER: I went to. . .*(Lowering his voice)*. . .take a leak.

EWEN: At Hattie's? *(Frantically)* Why there?

CHESTER: Well, I dunno. . .Let me see. It was raining. . .I couldn't wait.

EWEN: And so you went right to the back of the saloon and see him stabbing this other fellow.

CHESTER: I swear I did. Yes.

EWEN: Didn't other people notice it too. . .It's not in this paper, for instance. I've gone through it with a fine-tooth comb. *(He almost tears the newspaper to pieces.)* There are no murders mentioned in the paper. . .Just a few suicides. . .Oh, Chester, Chester, what is to become of you? *(Swiftly)* Did you take a leak when you got there, or just go spying?

CHESTER: Oh yes, I did that. . .*(shamed)* You see *(whispering again)* I saw the murder when I was. . .peeing. Through a hole in the wall. . .

EWEN: *(dazed)* I see. . .Go on.

CHESTER: But I dried my hands and come out into the room afterwards and he. . .was standing over the body.

EWEN: Well, didn't he see you.

CHESTER: I don't think so. . .I came like a shadow. He didn't look in my direction.

EWEN: Then what?

CHESTER: I hid behind a curtain that leads to the toilet.

James Purdy

EWEN: *(wildly) And,* Chester. . .*And?*

CHESTER: The man went in the toilet. . .He looked down in the bowl. . .*(Bemused)*

EWEN: Yes, yes!

CHESTER: He said, *Who pissed here? On account of I flushed it just a minute ago. Who has pissed here. . .*

EWEN: *(He suddenly puts his hand over* CHESTER'S *mouth as if to protect him.)* Oh, my God in heaven. . .

CHESTER: *(breaking away from the protecting hand)* I almost answered him back where I was hid behind the curtain. . .I was so mixed up, Ewen.

EWEN: But instead you said nothing.

CHESTER: I hid for an hour till all was quiet. *(EWEN holds him protectively.)* Then I went back in the room where he had done it, on account of the. . .stabber had flushed the toilet with the two. . .urines. . .*(EWEN puts his hand over* CHESTER'S *mouth.).* . .I. . .I. . .

EWEN: *(explosively)* But where were the other people all this while? Hattie, for example, where was she? You mean to say you were alone in that whole God-damned tavern?

CHESTER: Yes, because, they was having a drawing upstairs and everybod went up there for a few minutes to see who won. . . That was when the murderer struck. . .

EWEN: Look, we will go to Hattie's now, and we will ask around and find out. . .If you aren't telling me the truth, though, watch out. . .

CHESTER: Watch out for what? *(Terrified)* Watch out for what, Ewen.

EWEN: Nothing.

CHESTER: I know now I'm not lying. *(Stares at his brother's hands.)* I know the murderer.

EWEN: Well, that is big news.

CHESTER: *(moony)* But I imagined it, you see. . .Ewen *(terrified)*, there is a difference. . .I did take a. . .leak, but the rest of it, I must have imagined it. Tell me I did.

EWEN: Haven't I always been good to you, Chester, save a few times when I lost my temper. . .After all I have been both

48

mother and father to you. . .Haven't I been good to you for as long back as you can remember. I was already in the second grade when you were born. . .

CHESTER: I imagined it all, Ewen. . .After I went in the toilet. . .I just thought I saw a stabbing.

EWEN: *(strangely)* You're not afraid of me, are you, Chester. Chester.

CHESTER: I can't think. . .

EWEN: *(screaming)* See here! You must have known it was me all the time. . .Didn't you. See, I'm making a clean breast of it all. . .Look at me! You must have known I did it. . .

CHESTER: No, I didn't. . .No. . .Not till. . .

EWEN: Not till just. . .

CHESTER: A minute ago. When I saw your cut fingers. . .

EWEN: *(He looks at his own hands.)* Only a minute ago I was just your brother. . .

CHESTER: Are you going to do it to me to now, Ewen. . .Stab me too?

EWEN: Why ever would I do that to you?

CHESTER: I thought I would be next.

EWEN: You mean, Chester, you really didn't know it was me who stabbed him until just now. . .

CHESTER: I have never lied to you, Ewen. . .Sometimes I imagine, but never lie—because you are so close to me. . .

EWEN: Well, you used to make up things when you were little. . .Stories. . .you amused yourself telling stories.

CHESTER: Ewen, I will never tell on you. I am true. Maybe I make up stories from time to time because of my condition, but I am true.

EWEN: But why would you think I would kill you, Chester. . . That is a blow to me you think that. . .Anyhow, even if you told the police what you saw, nobody would believe you. . .

CHESTER: *(aroused)* Why ever not?

EWEN: *(bitterly)* Why ever not, he asks.

CHESTER: *(passionately)* Yes, why ever not, Ewen!

EWEN: *(He kisses him.)* You're not like other boys.

CHESTER: I'm like you, ain't I? Ain't I your own flesh and

blood, like you used to always tell me.

EWEN: Yes, but you're different too. That's precious.

CHESTER: No, no. I'm not different. I'm like you. . .You told me once. . .when I was. . .little that I would grow up to be like you too if I waited long enough.

EWEN: *(abstractedly, to himself really)* That was why I killed the man at Hattie's tavern. He mocked you. He mocked the way I kept such good care of you. . .*(Insanely)* He dared to question why I cared for you!

CHESTER: But you didn't believe what he said. . .about me. . .

EWEN: Of course not!

CHESTER: *(acting strange)* But see here. . .What exactly did he say about me. . .

EWEN: You be quiet now. . .We are going to pack and leave, hear? We're leaving New York City for good.

CHESTER: What did the man say about me, Ewen. . .You tell me.

EWEN: He didn't say a thing. *(He begins to put some clothes in a valise.)*

CHESTER: You tell me what he said. . .

EWEN: *(deliriously, forgetful anybody else is hearing)* He stung me! He stung me by his words. . .

CHESTER: So he did say it to you then? *(In violent collapse)*

EWEN: *(fearful)* No!

CHESTER: Who is the liar now? You tell me what he said because I am true, or—*(He shows the murder weapon to a terrifed EWEN.)* You must tell me because I am true. . .*(He waits.)* He spoke the truth against me, didn't he, Ewen?

EWEN: Put that knife away! That is a dangerous. . .

CHESTER: *(maniacally)* I am true, true. You should not have told me different. . .Admit it now, Ewen, that you have lied to me, that I will not grow up to be like you, though of the same flesh and blood. . .You have lied, and the man you murdered spoke true. . . See, see. . .*(He stabs EWEN in the throat again and again, and then pulling the blade out with difficulty he stabs himself.)*

EWEN: Here, here, Chester *(taking the knife)*. You have not done it quite, have you? *(He stabs* CHESTER *vehemently, then takes him in his arms.)* You stabbed me so good, but you failed on yourself. . .Such bright blood. . .Well, so what. . .It's better this way. . .You would have died anyhow with me in jail. . .*(He hugs him.)* Chester, Chester say I done good for you even if I did lie. . . Say I done good. . .Are you gone already? *(He rolls back the dead boy's eyes.)* Well, well. . .Dying is not all they write home about, is it? It's not any worse than life, that's sure. . .Chester, Chester. . Well, well. . .*(He dies.)*